To Gwen,
Love from Pam x
Christmas 2013.

DREAMS — Night and Day

Edited by

HUGH HELLICAR

PUBLISHED BY BEYOND THE CLOISTER PUBLICATIONS

Published by Beyond the Cloister Publications
1/14 Lewes Crescent
Brighton
East Sussex BN2 1FH
England

This collection copyright: © Hugh Hellicar 1995.

Copyright © of poems resides with individual authors.

No part of this publication may be reproduced, stored in a retrieval system, or transmitted in any form, or by any means, electronic, mechanical, photocopying, recording or otherwise, without the permission of the editor and authors.

The acknowledgements on page 143 consitute an extension of this copyright page.

ISBN 1 899605 05 3

Front Cover Design   Robert Tyndall

Design and Layout   Dorothy Steers

Typesetting, Artwork   Beyond the Cloisters Publications

Printed in Great Britian
by
J. W. Arrowssmith Ltd.
Bristol BS3 2NT

"We are the music-makers,
  And we are the dreamers of dreams",

Arthur O'Shaughnessy

INDEX

INTRODUCTION   15

PREFACE   19

INDEX OF POEMS   9

QUOTATIONS   14

DRAWINGS   21

POETS' BIOGRAPHICAL NOTES   139

ACKNOWLEDGEMENTS AND NOTES   143

INDEX OF POEMS

Matthew Arnold
    Longing   23
    A Question: To Fausta   24
    In Utrumque Paratus   25, 26

Richard Bauckham
    The Dream of Magi   27

William Blake
    The Angel   28

Emily Bronte
    A Day Dream   29, 32

Jeremiah Callanan
    The Outlaw of Loch Lene   33

Margaret Chisman
    Poem (Haiku)   34

Thomas Clarkson
    The Dreamer   35

Ross Clifford
    Epiphany   36
    The Leopard Skin Box   37, 38

Pamela Constantine
    Soul   39
    The Sighting   40

George Darling
    Nepenthe   41, 42

Fadma
    Journey   43

Rosemary Goring
    Huntsman   44

John Gurney
    Pit Widow   45, 46
    A Small Mourning   47, 48
    Pure Consciousness and
        the Silver Hill   49, 50

Ian Hallett
    Love Song   51
    On Visiting the Tomb of Freud   52
    October   53

Pamela Harvey
    To Isis   54

Hugh Hellicar
    Sleep Purpose Shared   56
    Dawn to Day   57

Robert Herrick
    The Dream   58
    The Vine   59

P. D. Isaac
    November   60

Eric James
    Fall and Rising   61- 63

Ben Jonson
    The Dream   64

John Keats
    To J.H. Reynolds Esq.   65- 67

William Kerr
    Counting Sheep   68

W. S. Landor
    Lines to a Dragon Fly   69

Reg. Latham
    What Could Be Stranger   70
    See Where Proud Night   71

James Mangan
    A Vision of Connaught
        in the 13th. Century   72- 74

Mary Frances Mooney
    Office Dreamer   75

Iris Munns
    Pre-Med   76

Arthur O'Shaughnessy
    Ode   77- 79

Edgar Allan Poe
    A Dream   80
    To—   81
    Dreams   82, 83

Jack Pollock
    Sma' Glen   84
    Legacy   85
    Sanctuary   86

Enoch Powell
    Poem (I Dreamt I saw)   88
    Poem (I Dreamt that on a Mountain)   89
    Poem (Dark over Staffordshire)   90
    Poem (I Dreamt I was in England)   91
    I Have Not Lost You   92

Maria Rajecka
    Reality   93

Kathleen Raine
    Soliloquies 3 and 4   94
    Soliloquies 9 and 11   95
    The Dream   96, 97
    Dream Landscapes 6   98

Helen Richards
    After Long years   99

Christina Rossetti
    Nursery Rhyme
        (Crying, my little one)   100
    Nursery Rhyme
        (I caught a little ladybird)   101
    Till Tomorrow   102
    Sonnet   103

Frederick Keeling Scott
    England   104

Percy Shelley
    Mutability   105

Mary Spain
  Sonnet (Dreamland) — 106
  Sonnet (A little garden) — 107
  Sonnet (A single dreaming heart) — 108
  Sonnet (This foolish dread) — 109

Derek Stanford
  The Heretic's Oneiric Petition — 110

Robert Louis Stevenson
  The Little Land — 112- 114
  Looking Forward — 115

Alfred, Lord Tennyson
  The Day Dream—Prologue — 116
  A Dream of Fair Women — 117- 121

R. S. Thomas
  Invitation — 122
  Night and Morning — 123
  The Face — 124, 125

Julie Whitby
  Solo Vision — 126
  Prayer — 127

Mary, Lady Wilson
  To Nostalgia — 129
  Manic-Depressive — 130

William Wordsworth
  Sonnet (Composed 1806) — 131
  Sonnet (Composed 1819) — 132

INDEX
OF
QUOTATIONS

ARTHUR O'SHAUGHNESSY	5
PERCY SHELLEY	17
WILLIAM WORDSWORTH	22
MATTHEW ARNOLD	55
EDGAR ALLAN POE	87
MARY, LADY WILSON	111
ENOCH POWELL	128
KATHLEEN RAINE	133

INTRODUCTION

Three sorts of dreams feature in this collection of poems; sleep dreams, day dreams and life dreams. The references to different forms of dreams so overlap that it seemed better to present the overall theme as dealt with by different poets.

How much we are motivated by dreams is a theme worked by Matthew Arnold, Reg Latham and others. Tennyson and Shelley imply that the poet is in a form of dream as he writes. How much anyone's life is built on a dream is hard to assess; but dreams of some sort relate to everyone's experience and this book will perhaps induce readers to wonder about the dream content of their own lives.

William Wordsworth's sonnet mentions both the pleasure and the fear found in dreams, and I am glad to include a poem referring to Dr. Freud by Ian Hallett. These poems are a reminder that some dreams are very personal, making many reticent to reveal them. For example, Emily Bronte was very reluctant to allow publication of her poems, and it seems important now to include the full version of her poem "A Day Dream" lest a false impression of her experience be given.

We are glad to include a good proportion of original work, notably two first publication poems by John Gurney; also "Fall and Rising" by Eric James, first heard in a sermon he gave this year. It is hard to imagine another modern poem that could more fully remind us of God's redemption from any dread experienced in dreams. He also quoted from Arthur O'Shaughnessy's poem "Ode"; We are the music-makers, and we are the dreamers of dreams". The full version is included.

Wherever possible the complete poem has been printed, especially where the poet's timespan of consent has passed.

The exceptions to this are "The Day Dream" by Lord Tennyson, which is marvellously long, and this shorter version does end suddenly, as a dream often does, when the good part is beginning. But in this case one can find out the ending. Also the passage from "Nepenthe" by George Darley is only a small part of the poem, which readers may be interested to trace in anthologies of Irish verse.

It is most pleasing to include poems by those whose work was especially appreciated in our last anthology "Poems of Faith and Love", Enoch Powell, Mary Spain, Jack Pollock and several more.

We welcome to this anthology Kathleen Raine, R.S. Thomas and Lady Wilson, whose poems have so often been highly valued at the public Poetry Readings by "Rainbows of Faith", with which we are associated. As dreams are a key part of life's mystery, an important feature of Kathleen Raine's poetry, her poems are a specially valued part of this collection. The depth of perception in R.S. Thomas' poems is as we expect; with several other contemporary poets included in these pages it is a treat to find.

Children's dreams are also included as these are relevant to us all, but regrettably we have only been able to include poets of the last century. These are R.L. Stevenson, William Blake, William Kerr, and nursery rhymes by Christina Rossetti.

We are most grateful to John James, a retired priest with a special interest in dreams, for writing a most appropriate Preface, which includes a poem, and encourages further reading.

Finally, I would like to thank those who have worked hard to bring this book into being.

28th. August 1995   Hugh Hellicar.

*"Peace, peace! he is not dead, he doth not sleep—
He hath awaked from the dream of life—"*

Percy Shelley.

PREFACE
REAL WORLD—OR DREAM -WORLD?

Life for many of us can sometimes seem very dream-like however grim the daily realities with which we have to deal. I am reminded of the Taoist story of Chuang Tzu, who dreamed one night that he was a butterfly. When he awoke, he found himself asking: "Am I Chuang Tzu dreaming that he is a butterfly? Or am I a butterfly dreaming that he is Chuang Tzu?".

Is it possible to take such thoughts seriously ? I think it is, for today all the challenges to our conventional world-view seem to come from a once-materialistic science.

Einstein, for instance, has taught us that things like *space* and *time* are at best mere concepts through which the human mind endeavours to interpret and make sense of its experience. That raises the question: Do we—or does part of us at least—live in a dimension *outside duration* where there is no past or future? Something that sees a larger picture of things because it is in touch with the Whole? That understanding would at least go some way towards explaining many of our more puzzling experiences—mysteries like foresight, telepathy and memories of past lives.

Again, we are all prone to think of our bodies as this *too—too—solid flesh*—though we may well sometimes wish, like Hamlet, *that some of it would melt*. Yet seen at the sub-atomic level through the modern electron-microscope, the body dissolves into a pulsating field of energy, vibrating to an individual pattern, in which a play of cells is continually being created and destroyed. Anything less *solid* would be hard to imagine. In other words, when seen from the heart of things, the individual is indivisible from the rest, the part is an expression of the whole. And what does that have to say about our ruthless intentions to *be myself* and *lead my own life*? Such insights can be mind-shattering, reducing us to total silence. Nothing remains but to "Be still and know that I am God"

Indeed, we sometimes speak of waking from our dreams with a certain sense of relief when we realise that it was *only a dream* and, to that extent, untrue or only partly true. But is it possible to *awaken* from the former life that we were leading as if from a dream, and to realise that hitherto our whole perspective on things has been very limited, if not entirely false?

I recently awoke from a dream, now forgotten, but with the following words running through my mind:

I glide along a stream
Where moon - blanched water lilies gleam
And subtle shadows hover deep below.

I wonder:
Is it all a dream?
And are things really what they seem
Or is there *something else* we do not know?

John M. James.

21

*"How sweet it is, When mother Fancy rocks
The waywood brain, to saunter through a wood"*

William Wordsworth

LONGING

Come to me in my dreams, and then
By day I shall be well again !
For then the night will more than pay
The hopeless longing of the day.

Come, as thou cam'st a thousand times,
A messenger from radiant climes,
A smile on thy new world, and be
As kind to others as to me!

Or, as thou never cam'st in sooth,
Come now, and let me dream it truth;
And part my hair, and kiss my brow,
And say: "My love! why sufferest thou?"

Come to me in my dreams, and then
By day I shall be well again!
For then the night will more than pay
The hopeless longing of the day.

                                      Matthew Arnold

A QUESTION
To Fausta

Joy comes and goes, hope ebbs and flows
Like the wave;
Change doth unknit the tranquil strength of men;
Love lends life a little grace,
A few sad smiles; and then,
Both are laid in one cold place,
In the grave.

Dreams dawn and fly, friends smile and die
Like spring flowers;
One vaunted life in one long funeral.
Men dig graves with bitter tears
For their dead hopes; and all,
Mazed with doubts and sick with fears,
Count the hours.

We count the hours ! These dreams of ours,
False and hollow,
Do we go hence and find they are not dead ?
Joys we dimly apprehend,
Faces that smiled and fled,
Hopes born here, and born to end,
Shall we follow ?

Matthew Arnold

IN UTRUMQUE PARATUS

If, in the silent mind of One all-pure,
    At first imagined lay
The sacred world; and by procession sure
From those still deeps, in form and colour drest,
Seasons alternating, and night and day,
The long-mused thought to north, south, east and west,
    Took then its all-seen way;

O waking on a world which thus-wise springs!
    Whether it needs thee count
Betwixt thy waking and the birth of things
Ages or hours—O waking on life's stream!
By lonely pureness to the all-pure fount
(Only by this thou canst) the colour'd dream
    Of life remount !

Thin, thin the plesant human noises grow,
    And faint the city gleams;
Rare the lone pastoral huts—marvel not thou!
The solemn peaks but to the stars are known,
But to the stars, and the cold lunar beams;
Alone the sun arises, and alone
    Spring the great streams.

But, if the wild unfather'd mass no birth
    In divine seats hath known;
In the blank, echoing solitude if Earth,
Rocking her obscure body to and fro,
Ceases not from all time to heave and groan,
Unfruitful oft, and at her happiest throe
    Forms, what she forms, alone;

O seeming sole to awake, thy sun-bathed head
    Piercing the solemn cloud
Round thy still dreaming brother-world outspread!
O man, whom Earth, thy long-vext mother, bare
Not without joy—so radiant, so endow'd
(Such happy issue crown'd her painful care)—
    Be not too proud!

Oh when most self-exalted most alone,
    Chief dreamer, own thy dream!
Thy brother-world stirs at thy feet unknown,
Who hath a monarch's hath no brother's part;
Yet doth thine inmost soul with yearning teem.
—Oh, what a spasm shakes the dreamer's heart !
    "I, too, but seem".

                              Matthew Arnold.

THE DREAM OF THE MAGI

They are asleep like us, under the same
motionless stars (out of the urban glare
starlight survives), wearily unaware
even of birth and death (Bethlehem became
Bosnia before they woke unrested). *Go*
(a blazing finger points) *this way. Beware*
(a distant lion roars) *the road you came.*
Home you will find the way you do not know

Richard Bauckham.

THE ANGEL

I Dreamt a Dream! what can it mean?
And that I was a maiden Queen,
Guarded by an Angel mild:
Witless woe was ne'er beguil'd !

And I wept both night and day,
And he wip'd my tears away,
And I wept both day and night,
And hid from him my heart's delight.

So he took his wings and fled;
Then the morn blush'd rosy red;
I dried my tears,and arm'd my fears
With ten thousand shields and spears.

Soon my Angel came again;
I was arm'd, he came in vain;
For the time of youth was fled
And grey hairs were on my head.

                    William Blake.

A DAY DREAM

On a sunny brae alone I lay
One summer afternoon;
It was the marriage-time of May
With her young lover, June.

From her Mother's heart seemed loath to part
That queen of bridal charms,
But her Father smiled on the fairest child
He ever held in his arms.

The trees did wave their plumy crests,
The glad birds carolled clear;
And I, of all the wedding guests,
Was only sullen there.

There was not one but wished to shun
My aspect void of cheer;
The very grey rocks, looking on,
Asked, "What do you do here?"

And I could utter no reply:
In sooth I did not know
Why I had brought a clouded eye
To greet the general glow.

So, resting on a heathy bank,
I took my heart to me;
And we together sadly sank
Into a reverie.

We thought, "When winter comes again,
Where will these bright things be?
All vanished, like a vision vain,
An unreal mockery?

The birds that now so blithely sing,
Through deserts frozen dry,
Poor spectres of the perished Spring
In famished troops will fly.

And why should we be glad at all?
The leaf is hardly green,
Before a token of the fall
Is on its surface seen".

Now whether it were really so
I never could be sure;
But as, in fit of peevish woe,
I stretched me on the moor.

A thousand thousand glancing fires
Seemed kindling in the air;
A thousand thousand silvery lyres
Resounded far and near:

Me thought the very breath I breathed
Was full of sparks divine,
And all my heather-couch was wreathed
By that celestial shine.

And while the wide Earth echoing rang
To their strange minstrelsy,
The little glittering spirits sang,
Or seemed to sing, to me:

'O mortal, mortal, let them die;
Let Time and Tears destroy,
That we may overflow the sky
With universal joy.

'Let Grief distract the sufferer's breast,
And Night obscure his way;
They hasten him to endless rest,
And everlasting day.

'To Thee the world is like a tomb,
A desert's naked shore;
To us, in unimagined bloom,
It brightens more and more.

"And could we lift the veil and give
One brief glimpse to thine eye
Thou would'st rejoice for those that live,
Because they live to die".

The music ceased—the noonday Dream
Like dream of night withdrew
But Fancy still will sometimes deem
Her fond creation true.

                                    Emily Bronte.

THE OUTLAW OF LOCH LENE

O many a day have I made good ale in the glen,
That came not of stream, or malt, like the brewing of men.
My bed was the ground, my roof, the greenwood above,
And the wealth that I sought—
                       one far kind glance from my love.

Alas! on that night when the horses I drove from the field,
That I was not near from terror my angel to shield.
She stretched forth her arms,—
                       her mantle she flung to the wind,
And swam o'er Loch Lene, her outlawed lover to find.

O would that a freezing sleet-winged tempest did sweep,
And I and my love were alonè far off on the deep!
I'd ask not a ship, or a bark, or pinnace to save,—
With her hand round my waist,
                       I'd fear not the wind or the wave.

'Tis down by the lake where the wild tree fringes its sides,
The maid of my heart, the fair one of Heaven resides—
I think as at eve she wanders its mazes along,
The birds go to sleep by the sweet wild twist of her song.

                                       Jeremiah Callanan.

POEM (HAIKU)

Open the shutters
Let the dawn work its magic
Store your dreams intact

Margaret Chisman

THE DREAMER

Beauty the butterfly
has alighted on her brow,
the plain girl fallen asleep.
Grave yet smiling,
of what is she dreaming?
She is beauty now.
No longer anonymous, dully pale,
touched by the ray of some invisible sun
her still face shines.
It must be love she is dreaming of—
she is a statue breathing, a madonna,
care has sunk like a stone.

Flowery, perfumed with sleep,
the trance stirs—
tendrils of fingers unclutch a sigh,
a blown rose falls from her breast.
Slowly the lips move,
make as to speak.

But I tiptoe away.
I would not hear that secret word,
that inviolable name.

      Thomas Clarkson

EPIPHANY

What Dreams
whisper to you in the early morning
when the glass vibrates with trams
     and the washboard sings—
Is it demons hungry for your flesh
in the room where far-off laughter's heard?
Is it that Wooded Landscape of 1727
by Thomas Gainsborough
     you saw in the Museum before closing?
I expect you know now—
but on waking, not: the far-off laughter gone;
the demons fled.

Your hair caught in my nail—
motorway of love,
cable to your heart, to dreams lost and found.
Your breathing is the only sound I hear—
to the pictures of your mind I have no key.

I seek those meadows and those groves
those deep-fretted brooks, that unopened rose.
I seek, and in seeking only get the silence,
no epiphany.

                              Ross Clifford

THE LEOPARD SKIN BOX

purple of fallen dreams
      of fantasy sleep
muted roses in a dark room
behind a slatted blind

the leap   into unconscious
was not very far
and yet I was an alien there

I was a shadow observed
a passage of time nervous
I was in the leopard skin box
So small
a fifty-pence insignificance
a screwed-up flag
was in there with me
     and a blue bow

I slept (upsidedown)
in a cloak of Venetian Red
in a leopard skin box.
One half in deep shadow
     hid my face and hands;

the smell of rotting
apples was my companion
although the blue was
unbearable
    the bird had died
pressed
into clay it lay light
in purple of fallen dreams, awaiting
to be waked to its destiny

                      Ross Clifford

SOUL

To my private garden
The white hart came,
Summoned by
A dreaming of his name;
His eyes were shy,
His form most proud, and he
Whispered, "It is shame
When soul must harden
In inferior frame".

Thus he from leafy cover
Summoned me
With gentle sigh
From sleeping memory,
Not asking why
I lingered in the dew:
Those eyes could see
With intensity of Lover,
And they knew.

                Pamela Constantine.

THE SIGHTING

Last night I saw
The Land I used to know
And the gossamer Gate
Through which I cannot go.

O sweet refinement
Of those weighted cells,
Transmute and keep me
Where my spirit dwells !

       Pamela Constantine

Nepenthe
(extract)

Over a bloomy land untrod
By heavier foot than bird or bee
Lays on the grassy-bosomed sod,
I passed one day in reverie.
High on this unpavilioned throne
The heaven's hot tyrant sat alone,
And like the fabled king of old
Was turning all he touched to gold.
The glittering fountains seemed to pour
Steep downwards rills of molten ore,
Grassily tinkling smooth between
Broom-shaded banks of golden green,
And o'er the yellow pasture straying
Dallying still yet undelaying,
In hasty trips from side to side
Footing adown their steepy slide
Headlong, impetuously playing
With the flowery border pied,
That edged the rocky mountain stair,
They pattered down incessant there,
To lowlands sweet and calm and wide.
With golden lip and glistening bell
Burned every bee-cup on the fell,
Whate'er its native unsunned hue,
Snow-white or crimson or cold blue;
Even the black lustres of the sloe
Glanced as they sided to the glow;

And furze in russet frock arrayed
With saffron knots, like shepherd maid,
Broadly tricked out her rough brocade.
The singed mosses curling here,
A golden fleece too short to shear!
Crumbled to sparkling dust beneath
My light step on that sunny heath.
Light, for the ardour of the clime
Made rare my spirit, that sublime
Bore me as buoyant as young Time
Over the green Earth's grassy prime,
Ere his slouch'd wing caught up her slime;
And sprang I not from clay and crime,
Had from those humming beds of thyme
Lifted me near the starry chime
To learn an empyrean rhyme.

O blest unfabled Incense Tree,
That burns in glorious Araby,
With red scent chalicing the air,
Till earth-life grow Elysian there!

                                        George Darley.

JOURNEY

—I saw you walking my way —
You are all my dreams.
              I am.
And I grew to love you;
You are now all my fears.
              I am.

                    fadma.

HUNTSMAN

And of the inmost mind,
Dim huntsman of its sleeping aviaries,
The running wisperer of its leaf-lit groves,
Stirrer of sybil shapes with hiding eyes:

Under what inner- cadenced streams
Of movement-dappled mood, or tenuous line
Of floating-stranded vision, do you pass ?
Under what water-wrinkled run of time ?

Not in the delicate futilities
Of crumbling dreams, their fluent flux and wane,
But in oblique listenings, footfalls not yet there,
Race of receding mirrors down the brain.

                                        Rosemary Goring

PIT-WIDOW

Odd, the way she absorbed her loss
into herself. It seemed that she possessed
him in a new way, took on his life, his cross,
his wholly different nature. She expressed
an interest in grass, and planted flowers.
Woke early every week-day, rose at five,
obedient to the hooter. Sat for hours
and listened to the fire. He seemed alive
within her, and his angers turned her own
like blackdamps, so she never felt alone.

Sometimes, as she slept, she worked his seams.
Still shuddered every time the rock fell in
and dropped into the gob. Each night her dreams
grew sharper, as, above the background din,
she'd focus on the creaking of the props'
quiet microtones. She knew however well-
positioned each one was, it could not stop
completely still. Odd runs of earth would tell
of roofs that had a tendency to slip,
compressed a chest, or pinioned a hip.

At times his spirit entered. Half-asleep,
exhausted by the deep and gassy pit,
it limped along the valley, then would creep
bewildered through the kitchen, quietly sit
slumped up before the fire-grate, slowly steam,
all coaly, in its pit-clothes. Silently
she'd ease him from his dark lethargic dream,
would peel away his shirt, methodically
strip off its greasy flannel. Make him lean,
black-leaded, for her hands to rub him clean.

She scrubbed away the coal-dirt, thick as tar,
from grime-filled cracks, and hollows, saw in turn
his blue wounds rematerialize, each scar
where stones had cut like bullets. Powder-burns
were outlined, then the contours of his ears
smashed flat by brawling colliers. Then, at last,
as filth oozed from his scalp, the skin came clear,
began to glint and glisten as she passed
her fingers through his hair-roots. Greyish-white,
each strand shone like a filament of light.

John Gurney.

A SMALL MOURNING

Somewhere here my surname is interred
in the black earth. It could be anywhere.
Near that old boarded chapel. By that absurd
cold monument. My eyes flick here and there,
examine texts. Their letters start to blur
like optical infections, show a strange
inventive desperation, yet confer
a dignity of sorts, an interchange
of rhetoric for death. The style is quaint.
Here every corpse is treated like a saint.

They'd kept, I think, no records. From the start
the child, half-turned, had come to go away.
Matrons quarrelled, kept his case apart
in corridors, agnosic. Small and grey
he came feet first, exhausted. Schopenhauer
might well have praised such absolute, austere
rejection of the Will. Alive an hour,
then over. An objectified idea.
Loveable in art, for contemplation.
Good to the impartial intuition.

That year the sewers froze. A shutter fell.
Snow settled, an oblivion. I forgot
particulars. It seems a burial
was held. But I was not invited, not
present. Common softwood, woolly, rough,
soon suffers from high shrinkage down the grain.
Divides with transverse fractures wide enough
for bones to show in hollows. For the brain
sets limits to suppression, cannot bind
forever all the violence of the mind.

These angels sway. Erratically displaced
by subsidence, they start to topple, fall.
One's staring, has a dull clay-coloured face
and a blank eye. Yes, I must hold a small
mourning. Sound the flat clank of a bell.
Reopen earth. Make something white descend
on ropes. Hear dirt fall, heavy, vertical
and ugly. Let things settle, have an end.
Even set a headstone, that will tilt
a memory of identity, of guilt.

                                      John Gurney.

PURE CONSCIOUSNESS
AND THE SILVER HILL

We sit apart, like quiet anchorites,
these lengthy winter minutes. Now our minds
are silenced as the black gangue of the night
is thickened in the east. For now we find
this simple self-possession. With delight
we feel no need for action, speak no word
to interrupt this soundless solitude,
this privacy each owns. Distinct, reborn,
with neither feeling vicious or absurd,
we wait here in this growing amplitude
with neither feeling absent or withdrawn.

The moon lifts from the distant silver hill.
Both also rest quite separate and apart,
yet each affirms the other, simple, still,
as if each used the practice, knew the art
of classical detachment, had the skill
of voiceless contemplation. Silently
the light accepts the shaft-dump, does not long
to penetrate, exploit, and then attack,
to tunnel in for metals, strive to be
in the Dreamer's Lode, Wheal Brothers'. Full and strong,
its beams define the engine-house, the stack.

The moon slips into cloud, but we have learned
to tolerate its absence, let it go,
well knowing that its circle will return,
its image will continue, still will glow
in grey transfiguration. Unconcerned,
we watch with mild amusement as the cloud
begins to fall apart, disintegrate,
to scatter like a black steam on the moor
then pass like transient blast-dust. Like a shroud
it breaks in fading pieces, dissipates
then drifts from our attention past the tor.

The light returns, we eye its form again.
No dread, no sudden crisis has begun.
Our bodies are not shattered, feel no pain
from muffled, deep implosions. Two, yet one,
we watch it shape the burrows, feel no strain,
require no special shining from a face
returning as a stranger's. All alarm
has vanished, long forgotten. Its caress
intensifies its blessing. Now its grace
is silvering our being, spreads this charm
of calm connatural love, pure consciousness.

John Gurney.

LOVE SONG

Years ago
in the deepest recesses of the night
I dreamed you, and your coming
was like the dawn breaking
on a familiar town.

But we have grown
hard with living,
you and I, and we must
act out our drama on
the steepest escarpments of the soul.

Always remember, darling,
that even when I fight you
I am loving you,
and only when you devour me
shall I be made whole.

      Ian Hallett.

ON VISITING THE TOMB OF FREUD

Truth was not enough, O Doctor of the Mind,
To shield you from the wrath of ignorant men,
When you inscribed with ready-flowing pen
The obscure dreams of perverse human-kind.
Too bold the seeker and too stark the find
To win a floral tribute for this tomb,
Here where the very winds are dumb
And all the stars seem blind.

Yet—could it be?—in far away Napal
Some goat-herd's wife knew of Love's secret land
All that you knew, but never wrote at all
Or spoke of it? Some, knowing, do not understand,
And other seekers, blinded by the small
Realities of life, no greater truths have scanned.

Ian Hallett

OCTOBER

This morning
I could smell the winter on the wind,
as I left you sadly regarding
a few grey hairs.
But now the cloudless afternoon
is lovelier than proud July !

How can I make you believe, my dear,
that the world shimmers with ecstacy
to the golden requiem of the leaves,
and that out in the blue-hazed distances
there comes a life again
all the long-lost dreams of youth?

And if you listen carefully
you will hear the low wind whisper:
"Remember, my darling,
all things beautiful
return".

        Ian Hallett

TO ISIS

Oh, how dark was the dawning of this Age
That gave my trembling wish its heritage;
In disillusion, doubt, a woman sad
Sought Life's elusive Wisdom lotus bud.

Now I look back and think along the way;
Perhaps it leads to bright and golden day—
Though mists of sorrow now the light shines clear
Though distant, showing ending to my fear.

But give me now the hope I offered you,
That my immortal dream may yet come true;
For I would share its meaning in this hour
With those who need assurance of its Power,
That from the Earthly seed I sowed can bloom
The glowing Sunflowers from an empty Tomb.

         Pamela Harvey

*"Come to me in my dreams, and then
By day I shall be well again"*.

Matthew Arnold

SLEEP PURPOSE SHARED

Daytime purpose, seen in looks,
Is never fully shared.
Sleep knows the other half,
Away from eyes and words,
And keeps some secret
From the woken self.

Sleep closely, and it's shared,
If half forgot before the dawn.

                                    Hugh Hellicar

DAWN TO DAY

I rest : she sleeps.
I dress my thoughts : she naked keeps
Her dreams hid.

Ardent glow still flows
In arms that reach
To touch her cheeks.
To wonder at her neck's sheen,
So white in the dawn light,
And plan the day
For her delight,
And pray
With new love
Is my delight.

To bring composure of the night
Into day,
Warm breath
Into cold air,
Time of giving
Into time of gain,
Only a fool would try,
And so do I.

                Hugh Hellicar

NOVEMBER

Seagulls hovering and lapping
The wind,
Then diving into the Humber.

The sky is grey but beyond
Appears lighter, as are my thoughts
Now you are behind me.

The snow will be coming soon.
Virgin white, as my heart will
Become again, as waiting for a
Flicker of a smile to return.

The sun will appear on these banks
Of hurt and bitter memory but
I shall remember you as free bird
Floating and singing then crying
With love.

                              P. D. Isaac

FALL AND RISING

Falling.
      Falling.
           Falling.
Falling for years and years.
Falling headlong,
Down
      into the shaft.
The slimy shining sides of the shaft
Glisten.
But there is only
      Falling.
           Falling.
                Falling.
Eventually,
      I have ceased to fall.
I have not "come to rest";
I lie in the slime,
At the bottom of the shaft.

A voice says: "Climb".
I lie silent,
Incapable of answer,
Or of movement.

The voice again says; "Climb".

I bestir myself,
And begin to climb.
But the walls are slime.
I seem to slip back further
Whenever I try to climb

There is a light
At the top of the shaft
That catches
The slimy sides of the shaft.

I climb—
So slowly,
So painfully.

The years of falling
Require
Answering years of climbing.

The light at the top of the shaft
Increases as I climb—
Blazes.
I long to reach the surface.

Eventually,
I heave myself
          into the light.

I lie there,
Exhausted,
In the light—
Just as I lay in the slime
At the bottom of the shaft—
Unable to move.

Gradually,
I am aware
I am within a room.

There is a table
              and candles.
The light is from the candles.
The light shines in the darkness.
There is Bread and Wine on the table.

It is the Lord
            at Supper,
With the Eleven.

And the Lord
Turns
And looks on me,
Smiles,
And says:
        "Come in, Judas.
           We couldn't finish without you."

                              Eric James.

THE DREAM

Or scorn, or pity on me take,
I must the true relation make,
I am undone tonight;
Love is a subtle dream disguised,
Hath both my heart and me surprised,
Whom never yet he durst attempt awake;
Nor will he tell me for whose sake
He did me the delight,
Or spite,
But leaves me to inquire,
In all my wild desire
Of sleep again; who was his aid;
And sleep so guilty and afraid,
As since he dares not come within my sight.

                                            Ben Jonson.

TO   J. H. REYNOLDS, ESQ.

Dear Reynolds,

           As last night I lay in bed,
There came before my eyes that wonted thread
of shapes, and Shadows and Remembrances,
That every other minute vex and please:
Things all disjointed come from North and South,
Two witch's eyes above a cherub's mouth,
Voltaire with casque and shield and Habergeon,
And Alexander with his night-cap on—
Old Socrates a tying his cravat;
And Hazlitt playing with Miss Edgworth's cat;
And Junius Brutus pretty well so so,
Making the best of 's way towards Soho.

Few are there who escape these visitings—
P 'rhaps one or two, whose lives have patent wings;
And through whose curtains peeps no hellish nose,
No wild boar tushes, and no Mermaid's toes:
But flowers bursting out with lusty pride;
And young Aeolian harps personified,
Some, Titian colours touch'd into real life.
The sacrifice goes on; the pontif knife
Gloams in the sun, the milk-white heifer lows
The pipes go shrilly, the libation flows:

A white sail shows above the green-head cliff
Moves round the point, and throws her anchor stiff.
The Mariners join hymn with those on land.—
You know the Enchanted Castle—it doth stand
Upon a Rock on the Border of a Lake
Nested in Trees, which all do seem to shake
From some old Magic like Urganda's sword.
O Phoebus that I had thy sacred word
To show this Castle in fair dreaming wise
Unto my friend, while sick and ill he lies.

You know it well enough, where it doth seem
A mossy place, a Merlin's Hall, a dream.
You know the clear lake, and the little Isles,
The Mountain blue, and cold near neighbour rills—
All which elsewhere are but half animate
Here do they look alive to love and hate;
To smiles and frowns; they seem a lifted mound
Above some giant, pulsing underground.

Part of the building was a chosen See
Built by a banished santon of Chaldee:
The other part two thousand years from him
Was built by Cuthbert of St. Aldebrim;
Then there's a little wing, far from the sun,
Built by a Lapland Witch turned maudlin nun—
And many other juts of aged stone
Founded with many a mason-devil's groan.

The doors all look as if they oped themselves,
The windows as if latch'd by fays and elves—
And from them comes a silver flash of light
As from the Westward of a summer's night;
Or like a beauteous woman's large blue eyes
Gone mad through olden songs and Poesies—

See what is coming from the distance dim!
A golden galley all in silken trim!
Three rows of oars are lightening moment-whiles
Into the verd'rous bosom of those Isles.
Towards the shade under the Castle Wall
It comes in silence—now 'tis hidden all.
The clarion sounds; and from a postern gate
An echo of sweet music doth create
A fear in the poor herdsman who doth bring
His breast to trouble the enchanted spring:
He tells of the sweet music and the spot
To all his friends, and they believe him not.

O that our dreamings all of sleep or wake
Would all their colours from the sunset take:
From something of material sublime,
Rather than shadow our own Soul's daytime
In the dark void of night. For in the world
We jostle—but my flag is not unfurl'd
On the Admiral staff—and to philosophize
I dare not yet !—Oh never will the prize,
High reason, and the lore of good and ill
Be my reward. Things cannot to the will
Be settled, but they tease us out of thought.
Or is it that Imagination brought
Beyond its proper bound, yet still confined,—
Lost in a sort of Purgatory blind,
Cannot refer to any standard law
Of either earth or heaven?—It is a flaw
In happiness to see beyond our bourn—
It forces us in Summer skies to mourn.
It spoils the singing of the Nightingale.

John Keats

COUNTING SHEEP

Half-awake I walked
A dimly-seen sweet hawthorn lane
Until sleep came;
I lingered at a gate and talked
A little with a lonely lamb.
He told me of the great still night,
Of calm starlight,
And of the lady moon, who'd stoop
For a kiss sometimes;
Of grass as soft as sleep, of rhymes
The tired flowers sang:
The ageless April tales
Of how, when sheep grow old,
As their faith told,
They went without a pang
To far green fields, where fall
Perpetual streams that call
To deathless nightingales.
    And then I saw, hard by,
A shepard lad with shining eyes,
And round him, gathered one by one
Countless sheep, snow-white;
More and more they crowded
With tender cries,
Till all the field was full
Of voices and of coming sheep.
Countless they came, and I
Watched, until deep
As dream-fields lie
I was asleep.

                William Kerr.

LINES TO A DRAGON FLY

LIFE (priest and poets say) is but a dream;
    I wish no happier one than to be laid
    Beneath some cool syringa's scented shade
Or wavy willow, by the running stream,
    Brimful of Moral, where the Dragon Fly,
    Wanders as careless and content as I.
Thanks for this fancy, insect king,
Of purple crest and filmy wing,
Who with indifference givest up
The water-lily's golden cup,
To come again and overlook
What I am writing in my book.
Believe me, most who read the line
Will read with hornier eyes than thine;
And yet their souls shall live for ever,
And thine drop dead into the river!
God pardon them, O insect king,
Who fancy so unjust a thing!

                    Walter Savage Landor.

WHAT COULD BE STRANGER ?

What could be stranger than the human mind ?
A cage for dreams, creation's nursery,
Curber of nature, curbed by destiny,
Selfless for truth, and self-deluded, blind.
What curious god, noble or mean, designed
That such a wavering point of strength should be
The fulcrum of a world so perilously,
On time's sheer edge, to life, to death, inclined.

This pregnant mind, that carries in its womb
The seed of good and evil, will it bear
In time to come perfect or monstrous fruit ?
Can its creator save it from the tomb
Of its own darkness, breed hope from despair,
Or shape an angel from potential brute?

Reg Latham

SEE WHERE PROUD NIGHT

See where proud night parades her stars
That come from dazzling distances to light
Our little world !
Are we so honoured in the universe
That all this concentrated majesty and power
But serve to our fulfillment ?
Are we indeed the flower and crown of life
Or a blind spot whose accidental birth
Will barely stir
The indifference of eternity ?
May there not be, beyond our climbing dream,
Far other worlds than this,
Where the heart has grown
To its full stature,
Where to corporeal grace
Thought adds new beauty,
Where delight may be
Wedded to wisdom ?
If life and time can breed such other men
Why should the power that bodies forth creation
Concern itself with us ?

Reg Latham

A VISION OF CONNAUGHT IN THE THIRTEENTH CENTURY

I walked entranced
  Through a land of Morn;
The sun, with wondrous excess of light,
  Shone down and glanced
  Over seas of corn
And lustrous gardens aleft and right
  Even in the clime
  Of resplendent Spain
Beams no such sun upon such a land;
  But it was the time,
  'Twas in the reign,
Of Cáhal Mór of the Wine-red Hand.

Anon stood nigh
  By my side a man
Of princely aspect and port sublime.
  Him queried I—
  'O, my Lord and Khan,
What clime is this, and what golden time?'
  When he—'The clime
  Is a clime to praise,
The clime is Erin's, the green and bland;
  And it is the time,
  These be the days,
Of Cáhal Mór of the Wine-red Hand!'

Then saw I thrones,
    And circling fires,
And a Dome rose near me, as by a spell,
    Whence flowed the tones
    Of silver lyres,
And many voices in wreathed swell;
    And their thrilling chime
    Fell on mine ears
As the heavenly hymn of an angel-band—
    'It is now the time,
These be the years,
Of Cáhal Mór of the Wine-red Hand!'

I sought the hall,
    And, behold!—a change
From light to darkness, from joy to woe!
    Kings, nobles, all,
    Looked agast and strange;
The minstrel-group sate in dumbest show!
    Had some great crime
    Wrought this dread amaze,
This terror? None seemed to understand
    'Twas then the time
    We were in the days,
Of Cáhal Mór of the Wine-red Hand.

I again walked forth,
   But lo! the sky
Showed fleckt with blood, and an alien sun
   Glared from the north,
And there stood on high,
Amid his shorn beams, a skeleton!
   It was by the stream
   Of the castled Maine,
One Autumn eve, in the Teuton's land,
   That I dreamed this dream
   Of the time and reign
Of Cáhal Mór of the Wine-red Hand !

                             James Mangan

OFFICE DREAMER

Fairy music haunts my sombre city days
Mocking smart decor, slick selling talk,
The swing of the sea under my brown boat
Wafting me away on the breast of a wave, rowing, rowing.
Rowing happily on an oceam of dreams;
Letters shoot out — I sell flats, shops, miles of concrete,
All done with the mind's remoter part,
The other part reclines on the great seas' heart;
Westward I roll towards pearly islands that divide sea and sky.
Mid-morn: Where, oh, where is my haven of peace?
The enchanted scene is dimmed by a haze,
Shrill seabirds drown all magic song,
The blue sky fades, a ceiling comes down on my reverie,
The mirage vanishes, reality pinions me.

         Mary Frances Mooney

PRE-MED

Shut away behind
close-drawn curtains,
I wince at the jab on my thigh—
which thrusts me out
on to an unknown sea;

voices are miles away
but I know they are there—
I hear other women laughing
and their words shuttle across
the ward, weaving a net

to carry me over sound;
my eyes watch the orderlies—
there is the click of metal
as the poles are threaded
through the sides of my stretcher;

this is a dream within a dream,
the voices are a sea of bubbles—
a frothy tide for me to drown in
as they wheel me into the theatre
where the real performance begins.

Iris Munns.

ODE

We are the music-makers,
    And we are the dreamers of dreams,
Wandering by lone sea-breakers,
    And sitting by desolate streams;—
World-losers and world forsakers,
    On whom the pale moon gleams:
Yet we are the movers and shakers
    Of the world for ever, it seems.

With wonderful deathless ditties
we build up the world's great cities,
    And out of a fabulous story
    We fashion an empire's glory:
One man with a dream, at pleasure,
    Shall go forth and conquer a crown;
And three with a new song's measure
    Can trample a kingdom down.

We, in the ages lying
    In the buried past of the earth,
Built Nineveh with our sighing,
    And Babel itself in our mirth;
And o'erthrew them with prophesying
    To the old of the new world's worth;
For each age is a dream that is dying,
    Or one that is coming to birth.

A breath of our inspiration
Is the life of each generation;
    A wondrous thing of our dreaming,
    Unearthly, impossible seeming—
The soldier, the king, and the peasant,
    Are working together in one,
Till our dreams shall become their present,
    And their work in the world be done.

They had no vision amazing
Of the goodly house they are raising;
    They had no divine foreshowing
    Of the land to which they are going:
But on one man's soul it had broken,
    A light that doth not depart;
And his look, or a word he had spoken,
    Wrought flame in another man's heart.

And therefore to-day is thrilling
With a past day's late fulfilling;
    And the multitudes are enlisted
    In the faith that their fathers resisted,
And, scorning the dream of to-morrow,
    Are bringing to pass, as they may,
In the world, for its joy or its sorrow,
    The dream that was scorned yesterday.

But we, with our dreaming and singing,
    Ceaseless and sorrowless we!
The glory about us clinging
    Of the glorious futures we see,
Our souls with high music ringing:
    O men! it must ever be
That we dwell, in our dreaming and singing,
    A little apart from ye.

For we are afar with the dawning
    And the suns that are not yet high,
And out of the infinite morning
    Intrepid you hear us cry—
How, spite of your human scorning,
    Once more God's future draws nigh,
And already goes forth the warning
    That ye of the past must die.

Great hail! we cry to the comers
    From the dazzling unknown shore;
Bring us hither your sun and your summers,
    And renew our world as of yore;
You shall teach us your song's new numbers,
    And things that we dreamed not before:
Yea, in spite of a dreamer who slumbers,
    And a singer who sings no more.

                      Arthur O'Shaughnessy.

A DREAM

In visions of the dark night
   I have dreamed of joy departed;
But a waking dream of life and light
   Hath left me broken-hearted.

Ah! what is not a dream by day
   To him whose eyes are cast
On things around him, with a ray
   Turned back upon the past ?

That holy dream, that holy dream,
   While all the world were chiding,
Hath cheered me as a lovely beam
   A lonely spirit guiding.

What through that light, thro' storm and night,
   So trembled from afar—
What could there be more purely bright
   In Truth's day-star?

                    Edgar Allan Poe.

TO—

The bowers whereat, in dreams, I see
   The wantonest singing birds,
Are lips—and all thy melody
   Of lip-begotten words—

Thine eyes, in Heaven of heart enshrined
   Then desolately fall,
O God ! on my funereal mind
   Like starlight on a pall—

Thy heart—*thy* heart !—I wake and sigh,
   And sleep to dream till day
Of the truth that gold can never buy—
   Of the baubles that it may.

                      Edgar Allan Poe.

DREAMS

Oh! that my young life were a lasting dream!
My spirit not awakening, till the beam
Of an Eternity should bring the morrow.
Yes! though that long dream were of hopeless sorrow,
'Twere better than the cold reality
Of waking life, to him whose heart must be,
And hath been still, upon the lovely earth,
A chaos of deep passion, from his birth.
But should it be—that dream eternally
Continuing—as dreams have been to me
In my young boyhood—should it thus be given,
'Twere folly still to hope for higher Heaven.
For I have revelled when the sun was bright
I' the summer sky, in dreams of living light
And loveliness—have left my very heart
In climes of mine imagining apart?
From mine own home, with beings that have been
Of mine own thought—what more could I have seen?
'Twas once—and only once—and the wild hour
From my remembrance shall not pass—some power
Or spell had bound me—'twas the chilly wind
Came o'er me in the night, and left behind
Its image on my spirit—or the moon
Shone on my slumbers in her lofty noon
Too coldly—or the stars—howe'er it was
That dream was as that night-wind—let it pass.

I have been happy—and I love the theme:
Dreams ! in their vivid colouring of life
As in that fleeting, shadowy, misty strife
Of semblance with reality which brings
To the delirious eye, more lovely things
Of Paradise and Love—and all my own !—
Than young Hope in his sunniest hour hath known.

> Edgar Allan Poe.

SMA' GLEN

From this small place
the earth called out
come, share your early love
and I will give full measure in return.

Here golden warriors from the north made fire
to form bronze ploughshares from the galley's head
and shared my many harvests.

Tired rebels found their peace among my rushes
and missed the carnage of Culloden's field
the crowded impotence of a hero's churchyard
and requiems in barley for the brave.

The willow tree beside that shaded pool
has stood against the sun a hundred years
to keep a dim secluded trysting place
for silver lovers at their journey's end.

Soon there will be a season of white silence
when restless dogs will blame the winter moon
as yellow spring comes bending in the meadow
last summer's seed will find this place again.

                                        Jack Pollock.

LEGACY

I dreamed that
you still lived,
we lay together
one beside the other.
You spoke of children
and the future—
ripe with promise.

I woke when dawn
was colouring the hill
where you lie now,
changing your form
to nourish the earth
and feed the cherry tree
that stands above
your resting place,
and every spring
your blossom scents the air.

                    Jack Pollock.

SANCTUARY

I could settle here
and make concessions
to approaching winter.
Those high windows stand
between me and everything—
I seem to need to
heal my wounded head.
Up there is a chance
to live like other people
clean sheets on bed,
white knickers in the bathroom.
Here on the street, straining
like a pirahna against the
windows of my Porsche,
the light cannot reach me.
If I could still my dreams and aspirations
and stem the torrent of my discontent,
I could climb the stairs and lie comfortably—
in the warmth of her claws.

Jack Pollock

"That holy dream, that holy dream,
While all the world were chiding".

Edgar Allan Poe

POEM

I DREAMT I saw with waking eyes the scene
    So often in imagination wrought,
The flame-wall in the night at Alamein
    Before the attack. And I was glad, and thought:
"My sorrow and despair was after all
    Some evil dream. It still is not too late,
My friends who passed before me through that wall
    Not lost, nor I for ever separate
From them condemned to live. I break to-night
    As they did through the fire, and so again,
Knowing and known, shall pass into their sight."
    But then I woke, and recollection came
That I for ever and alone remain
    On this side of the separating flame.

Enoch Powell.

POEM

I DREAMT that on a mountain-crest
As in the sheep-cropped grass we lay,
The words that ever at my breast
Leap and are striving to be spoke
Suddenly I began to say.
Yet words not those I purposed
From lips amd heart impassioned broke
But, as it seemed to me, I said:
"Therefore with all archangels I,
All angels and Heaven's company
Thy glorious name
Do magnify,
Thee praising and for evermore
Saying—" and from your mouth reply
Not such as that I waited for
In whispered tones mysterious came
But—"Holy Thou, of hosts the Lord,
Full of Thy glory earth and sky,
Glory to Thee,
O God most high!"
You ceased. The wind that through the sward
With steady-breathing passion swept,
From flower and grass and heather blent
"Amen" to that strange sacrament;
And silent, as it seemed, we wept.

                              Enoch Powell.

POEM

Dark over Staffordshire lie bent
   The heavy clouds;
By banks of Penk, and Sow, and Trent
   In dank, dim shrouds
Dawn mists are creeping
   Out of the gloom
Where she is sleeping
Whose heart is keeping
   Hidden my doom.

Pale over Cannock Chase the light
   Slowly appears,
Which ends for ever the long night
   Of dreams and fears.
Be what it send me
   Desire or hate,
Arise, befriend me,
Crown me or end me,
   Sun of my fate!

              Enoch Powell.

POEM

I DREAMT I was in England
   And heard the cuckoo call,
And watched an English summer
   From spring to latest fall,
   And understood it all.

I dreamt my feet were dusty
   With dust of English lanes,
From walking through the counties
   And healing of my pains
   With summer suns and rains.

I dreamt the war was over
   And England strong and free,
And I lay there in England
   Beneath a broad yew-tree,
   Contented there to be.

                Enoch Powell.

I HAVE NOT LOST YOU

I have not lost you; where you've been
You still remain, unknown, unseen;
And I'll possess you everywhere,
                If I but dare.

Upon the field of battles lost
And on the barren ocean tossed—
In all my days of dull despair,
                I'll have you there.

And when the mind is large and free
In laughter or in victory,
I'll call your spirit from the air,
                And you shall share.

                              Enoch Powell.

REALITY

You speak about your dream—
about the Abstract Reality.
It is a contradiction in terms,
but yet it makes sense.
It takes you away from your
surroundings into
The World of Heaven.
You hear God's command,

The Word,

because it is the only
word spoken by Him for us.
You know it—
Deep inside you
there is a dream of Paradise,
and the Word—
the Word is the pass.
Dream,   dream again
and it will come—in silence—
from Him to you,
and all your life
will be insignificant
except for the Word of God.

                    Maria Rajecka

SOLILOQUIES

III

I wake to the familiar from the unknown
Dream-places where I also am, as they
Dwindle and submerge; all day
In this familiar room
I have been struggling to climb
A hill of sliding wave-worn stones innumerable;
Who, and where, am I ?

IV

That I of dream
Carries the burden of the one I am.
And was. Time
Is inexorable, all that has been
Is here and now, and is to come.

Kathleen Raine.

SOLILOQUIES

IX
I set out in a dream
To go away—
Away is hard to go, but no one
Asked me to stay,
And there is no destination
For away.

XI
What dreamer dreams my life-long quest ?
Why must heart soar, and mind
Seek what is high and far ?
Travelling a world of wonders have I lost or found
What is dear and near ?

Kathleen Raine.

THE DREAM

What land is native to us but a dream
We have told one another, leaf by leaf,
Golden bough and golden flower,
Fountain and tree and stream,
That Paradise unseen

Its unheard music we have sung
Lover to lover,
In sunlit glades we have depicted Her,
Our Eve, our Primavera,
And sweet Virgin Mary with all her babes,

Whose bliss is ours—not that our fingers played
With strand of golden hair
Or reach for that ripe fruit
She offers, or lily-flower,
Holy mother to holy child,

But we have made it so—
Those angels, sinless saints,
Souls who, purified by death,
Dwell in our images for ever, neither come
Nor go from that imagined place.

We, who have loved and known
Beauty only as we have traced those presences
Robed and adorned with beyond-price jewels
Of our imagining

Is it that we are
Semblances in the enactment of a dream
That dreams us, life by shadowy life
In Eden, under those bright boughs
Beside that flowing stream?

                              Kathleen Raine.

DREAM LANDSCAPES

VI

In a dream I was a stranger
In the small house of a follower
Of William Blake, who once lived there.

Outside, a cottage border
Of summer flowers I used to grow,
Among them, Jocob's Ladder.

Dreams slip in unawares
Their messages, and I woke remembering
Angels ascending and descending.

        Kathleen Raine.

AFTER LONG YEARS

After long years
Of unadmitted fear,
From the dark cave
Wherein I dream,
I come at last—
Bemused by the magic beam.

This golden , hard, unlikely soil
Yet bids me dig for treasure.
I take a spade—
Unseemly tool for woman's hand—
And dig for treasure, deep.

And now the earth feels soft and warm,
I do not see
It's but the sharpness of my eager tool
That makes it soft.
The sweet warmth
Comes from my own joyous labours.
Earth is cold.
With sharp delight, into my pit I leap,
And dig my prison deep.

                              Helen Richards

A NURSERY RHYME
Crying, my little one,

Crying, my little one, footsore and weary?
   Fall asleep, pretty one, warm on my shoulder:
I must tramp on through the winter night dreary,
   While the snow falls on me colder and colder.

You are my one, and I have not another;
   Sleep soft, my darling, my trouble and treasure;
Sleep warm and soft in the arms of your mother,
   Dreaming of pretty things, dreaming of pleasure.

Christina Rossetti.

A NURSERY RHYME
I caught a little ladybird

I caught a little ladybird
  That flies far away;
I caught a little lady wife
  That is both staid and gay.

Come back, my scarlet ladybird,
  Back from far away;
I weary of my dolly wife,
  My wife that cannot play.

She's such a senseless wooden thing
  She stares the livelong day;
Her wig of gold is stiff and cold
  And cannot change to grey.

                Christina Rossetti.

TILL TOMORROW

Long have I longed, till I am tired
   Of longing and desire;
Farewell my points in vain desired,
   My dying fire;
Farewell all things that die and fail and tire.

Springtide and youth and useless pleasure
   And all my useless scheming,
My hopes of unattainable treasure,
   Dreams not worth dreaming,
Glow-worms that gleam but yield no warmth in gleaming,

Farewell all shows that fade in showing:
   My wish and joy stand over
Until tomorrow; Heaven is glowing
   Thro' cloudy cover,
Beyond all clouds loves me my Heavenly Lover.

Christina Rossetti.

SONNET

A dream there is wherein we are fain to scream,
While struggling with ourselves we cannot speak:
And much of all our waking life, as weak
And misconceived, eludes us like the dream.
For half life's seemings are not what they seem,
And vain the laughs we laugh, the shrieks we shriek;
Yea, all in vain that mars the settled meek
Contented quiet of our daily theme.
When I was young I deemed that sweets are sweet:
But now I deem some searching bitters are
Sweeter than sweets, and more refreshing far,
And to be relished more, and more desired,
And more to be pursued on eager feet,
On feet untired, and still on feet tho' tired.

Christina Rossetti.

ENGLAND

To the grunt and rattle and jolt on the train
On our hearts there beat a long refrain
As we view old England once again—

    "We fought for you"

The trim cut hedges slipping by,
The village church towers lifted high,
And over all an English sky—

    "We fought for you"

The little kiddies out from school,
The cattle drinking at the pool,
The squire, the parson and village fool,

    "We fought for you"

We fought but cannot fight again
For the past looms through a mist of pain,
But a big content lies in the strain

    "We fought—for you"

                  Frederick Keeling Scott

MUTABILITY

The flower that smiles to-day
    To-morrow dies;
All that we wish to stay
    Tempts and then flies.
What is this world's delight ?
Lightning that mocks the night,
    Brief even as bright.

Virtue, how frail it is!
    Friendship how rare!
Love, how it sells poor bliss
    For proud despair!
But we, though soon they fall,
Survive their joy, and all
    Which ours we call.

Whilst skies are blue and bright,
    Whilst flowers are gay,
Whilst eyes that change ere night
    Make glad the day;
Whilst yet the calm hours creep,
Dream thou—and from thy sleep
    Then wake to weep.

                Percy Shelley.

DREAMLAND

Men stand and dream upon a Sussex hill,
Intent on powerful shoulders, flying feet,
In search of that tenacity of will
Which gives a colt the courage to compete
In classic company. Untroubled by
This burden of high hopes—and unaware
Of former equine heroes that supply
Their youthful speed and stamina—a pair
Of two year-olds burst gaily up the slope
And thunder past. As distant hoofbeats fade
Binoculars are lowered; with fresh hope
New dreams are fabricated, new plans laid.
Such heady dreams; perhaps, all said and done,
The colts know best who simply race for fun.

Mary Spain

A LITTLE GARDEN

On summer afternoons, from two to four,
The sunshine's probing fingers gently trace
A passage 'twixt the city roofs to pour
In fullness on a basement dwelling place.
Here, tended by the occupant within,
A little garden manages to grow.
Each corner for a pot or earth filled tin
Is utilised; and from these efforts flow
Such unexpected Summer flowers that we
Who pass, heads bent and lost in thought, for this
Brief moment waken from our dreams to see
A world made brighter by such loveliness.
A little garden? No ! My heart denies
That such a paradise be judged by size.

                                    Mary Spain.

A SINGLE DREAMING HEART

Long shadows on the grass proclaim the dawn,
The winter is but herald to the spring;
From out of death is hope of life reborn,
From out of sleep must come awakening.
Without the darkness who can speak of light ?
Can man know hope who has not known despair;
Or, without any option, choose the right;
Or, without isolation, learn to share ?
If black and white as matching halves are seen,
And pain and pleasure cannot live apart,
Duality's apparent coloured screen
Dissolves to show creation's single heart.
A single dreaming heart that peoples space
With all the fantasies of time and place.

                                                Mary Spain.

THIS FOOLISH DREAD

I wake to total blackness. Senses reel
In blind, consuming panic whilst my feet—
In service to this fear—kick off the sheet
And stumble to the window. Quick! Peel
Aside the curtains, let the night reveal
At very least a star. At last ! As heat
Of terror cools to quietude I greet
With weary joy the moon's pale beam that steals
Through scudding clouds to bring the sought-for light.
Where were you, light of reason, that you shed
No sense upon these phantoms of the night ?
Calm light of truth, dispel this foolish dread.
Come, let your brilliance put fear to flight
And guide me, quietened, to my waiting bed.

                                    Mary Spain.

THE HERETIC'S ONEIRIC PETITION

Madonna, Mary, Mother born of Eve,
I thank you for my sleep's munificence.
The dawn is grey. Return me to my dreams.

It's not yet day—the day and all it means.
I light a candle to you in my mind.
Light of the dawn, return me to my dreams.

You, with your poem the Magnificat,
know well what praise and glory I intend,
but words, alas, are all—too—wayward things.

Outside, I hear the milk's delivery.
The puppy barks next door, disgruntledly.
With day half-grown, return me to my dreams.

From frets, impatience, wry anxieties,
the urge to work without the energy,
deliver me. Return me to my dreams.

Meanwhile, in lieu of prayer, accept these crumbs,
these orts and rheumy-eyed apologies—
heart-meant—though ill-becoming they may seem.

Till your day breaks for me, restore my dreams.

Derek Stanford

*"Dim and unreal the present always seemed
 Until I saw it mirrored once again"*

Mary Wilson

THE LITTLE LAND

When at home alone I sit
And am very tired of it,
I have just to shut my eyes
To go sailing through the skies—
To go sailing far away
To the pleasent Land of Play;
To the fairy land afar
Where the Little People are;
Where the clover-tops are trees.
And the rain-pools are the seas,
And the leaves like little ships
Sail about on tiny trips;
And above the daisy tree
    Through the grasses,
High o'erhead the Bumble Bee
    Hums and passes.

In that forest to and fro
I can wander, I can go;
See the spider and the fly,
And the ants go marching by
Carrying parcels with their feet
Down the green and grassy street.
I can in the sorrel sit
Where the ladybird alit.
I can climb the jointed grass;
    And on high
See the greater swallows pass
    In the sky,
And the round sun rolling by
Heeding no such things as I.

Through that forest I can pass
Till, as in a looking glass,
Humming fly and daisy tree
And my tiny self I see
Painted very clear and neat
On the rain-pool at my feet.
Should a leaflet come to land
Drifting near to where I stand,
Straight I'll board that tiny boat
Round the rail-pool sea to float.

Little thoughtful creatures sit
On the grassy coasts of it;
Little things with lovely eyes
See me sailing with surprise.
Some are clad in armour green—
(These have sure to battle been!)—
Some are pied with ev'ry hue,
Black and crimson, gold and blue;
Some have wings and swift are gone;—
But they all look kindly on.

When my eyes I once again
Open, and see all things plain:
High bare walls, great bare floor;
Great big knobs on drawer and door;
Great big people perched on chairs
Stitching tucks and mending tears,

Each a hill that I could climb,
And talking nonsense all the time—
　　O dear me,
　　That I could be
A sailor on the rain-pool sea,
A climber in a clover tree,
And just come back, a sleepy-head,
Late at night to go to bed.

　　　　　　　　　　Robert Louis Stevenson.

LOOKING FORWARD

When I am grown to man's estate
I shall be very proud and great,
And tell the other girls and boys
Not to meddle with my toys.

                    Robert Louis Stevenson.

THE DAY-DREAM
Prologue

O Lady Flora, let me speak:
    A pleasant hour has past away
While, dreaming on your damask cheek,
    The dewy sister-eyelids lay.
As by the lattice you reclined,
    I went thro' many wayward moods
To see you dreaming—and, behind,
    A summer crisp with shining woods.
And I too dream'd, until at last
    Across my fancy, brooding warm,
The reflex of a legend past,
    And loosely settled into form.
And would you have the thought I had,
    And see the vision that I saw,
Then take the broidery-frame, and add
    A crimson to the quaint Macaw,
And I will tell it. Turn your face,
    Nor look with that too-earnest eye—
The rhymes are dazzled from their place,
    And order'd words asunder fly.

                          Alfred, Lord Tennyson.

A DREAM OF FAIR WOMEN

I read, before my eyelids dropt their shades,
    "The Legend of Good Women," long ago
Sung by the morning star of song, who made
    His music heard below;

Dan Chaucer, the first warbler, whose sweet breath
    Preluded those melodious bursts that fill
The spacious times of great Elizabeth
    With sounds that echo still.

And, for a while, the knowledge of his art
    Held me above the subject, as strong gales
Hold swollen clouds from raining, tho' my heart,
    Brimful of those wild tales,

Charged both mine eyes with tears. In every land
    I saw, wherever light illumineth,
Beauty and anguish walking hand in hand
    The downward slope to death.

Those far-renowned brides of ancient song
    Peopled the hollow dark, like burning stars,
And I heard sounds of insult, shame, and wrong,
    And trumpets blown for wars;

And clattering flints batter'd with clanging hoofs:
    And I saw crowds in column'd sanctuaries;
And forms that pass'd at windows and on roofs
    Of marble palaces;

Corpses across the threshold; heroes tall
    Dislodging pinnacle and parapet
Upon the tortoise creeping to the wall;
    Lances in ambush set;

And high shine-doors burst thro' with heated blasts
    That run before the fluttering tongues of fire;
White surf wind-scatter'd over sails and masts,
    And ever climbing higher;

Squadrons and squares of men in blazen plates,
    Scaffolds, still sheets of water, divers woes,
Ranges of glimmering vaults with iron grates,
    And hush'd seraglios.

So shape chased shape as swift as, when to land
    Bluster the winds and tides the self-same way,
Crisp foam-flakes scud along the level sand,
    Torn from the fringe of spray.

I started once, or seem'd to start in pain,
    Resolved on noble things, and strove to speak,
As when a great thought strikes along the brain,
    And flushes all the cheek.

And once my arm was lifted to hew down
    A cavalier from off his saddle-bow,
That bore a lady from a leaguer'd town;
    And then, I know not how,

All those sharp fancies, by down-lapsing thought
    Stream'd onwards, lost their edges, and did creep
Roll'd on each other, rounded, smooth'd, and brought
    Into the gulfs of sleep.

At last methought that I had wander'd far
    In an old wood: fresh-wash'd in coolest dew,
The maiden splendours of the morning star
    Shook in the steadfast blue.

Enormous elm-tree-boles did stoop and lean
    Upon the dusty brushwood underneath
their broad curved branches, fledged with clearest green,
    New from its silken sheath.

The dim red morn had died, her journey done,
    And with dead lips smiled at the twilight plain,
Half-fall'n across the threshold of the sun,
    Never to rise again.

There was no motion in the dumb dead air,
    Not any song of bird or sound of rill;
Gross darkness of the inner sepulchre
    Is not so deadly still

As that wide forest. Growths of jasmine turn'd
    Their humid arms festooning tree to tree,
And at the root thro' lush green grasses burn'd
    The red anemone.

I knew the flowers, I knew the leaves, I knew
    The tearful glimmer of the languid dawn
On those long, rank, dark wood-walks drench'd in dew,
    Leading from lawn to lawn.

The smell of violets, hidden in the green,
    Pour'd back into my empty soul and frame
The times when I remember to have been
    Joyful and free from blame.

And from within me a clear under-tone
    Thrill'd thro' mine ears in that unblissful clime,
"Pass freely thro': the wood is all thine own,
    Until the end of time."

At length I saw a lady within call,
    Stiller than chisell'd marble, standing there;
A daughter of the gods, divinely tall,
    And most divinely fair.

Alfred, Lord Tennyson.

INVITATION

And one voice says: Come
Back to the rain and manure
Of Siloh, to the small talk,
Of the wind, and the chapel's

Temptation; to the pale
Sickly half-smile of
The daughter of the village
Grocer. The other says: Come

To the streets, where the pound
Sings and the doors open
To its music, with life
Like an express train running

To time. And I stay
Here, listening to them, blowing
On the small soul in my
Keeping with such breath as I have.

       R.S. Thomas.

NIGHT AND MORNING

One night of tempest I arose and went
Along the Menai shore on dreaming bent;
The wind was strong, and savage swung the tide,
And the waves blustered on Caernarfon side.

But on the morrow, when I passed that way,
On Menai shore the hush of heaven lay;
The wind was gentle and the sea a flower,
And the sun slumbered on Caernarfon tower.

R.S. Thomas.

(From the Welsh Traditional)

THE FACE

When I close my eyes, I can see it,
That bare hill with the man ploughing,
Corrugating that brown roof
Under a hard sky. Under him is the farm,
Anchored in its grass harbour;
And below that the valley
Sheltering its few folk,
With the school and the inn and the church,
The beginning, middle and end
Of their slow journey above ground.

He is never absent, but like a slave
Answers to the minds bidding,
Endlessly ploughing, as though autumn
Were the one season he knew.
Sometimes he pauses to look down
To the grey farmhouse, but no signals
Cheer him; there is no applause
For his long wrestling with the angel
Of no name. I can see his eye
That expects nothing, that has the rain's
Colourlessness. His hands are broken
But not his spirit. He is like bark
Weathering on the tree of his kind.

He will go on; that much is certain.
Beneath him tenancies of the fields
Will change; machinery turn
All to noise. But on the walls
Of the mind's gallery that face
With the hills framing it will hang
Unglorified, but stern like the soil.

                                    R.S. Thomas.

SOLO VISION

Those old school gates are ahead of us now
as we linger in the back of the car:
my father, darkly handsome gypsy-fashion,
tells me he's mentioned in Mayakovsky,
"Solo Vision," or something like that.
He's mildly pleased. Would I like some fruit ?
My hug is clumsy, affectionate. But then I see

A too-huge moon whose brilliance terrifies—
striking that mortality chord as surely as a clock.
"Oh I never get tired" he smiles, looking shyly wise.
Perhaps he'll make ninety? Or beyond. I'm unaware
this is merely a dream, if beautiful, rare—
I rejoice at the chance of his company again.

                                              Julie Whitby.

PRAYER

Send me sleep, gentle as pollen in the wind.
Let the tireless galloping of mind cease.
Mind grandly, miraculously turned
Tchaikovsky's first concerto!
Allow my swans tomorrow will be geese.
Let me find the soft pedal soon
before décolleté night, replete with attractive vices—
her garlic and cinnamon spices—
corrupts as she caresses, disintegrates.
Let me quietly unwind her fleece in dreams.
Cool sleep, decend.

Julie Whitby.

*"I Dreamt I was in England
And heard the cuckoo call"*

Enoch Powell

TO NOSTALGIA

You first enthralled me in my early days
Almost before my babyhood was gone;
All through my life, to show the light which shone
Brilliant and clear, on days through which I'd dreamed
And scarcely felt life's happiness and pain;
Dim and unreal the present always seemed
Until I saw it mirrored once again.
But now, I try to grasp each passing day,
Yet, as the shadows gather, I suspect
That, in the magic of your spell, I may
Have lived my muddled life in retrospect;
And I am troubled by the fear that I
Like Lot's wife, looking back, may petrify.

Mary Wilson

MANIC—DEPRESSIVE

Today when I awakened to the light,
I knew that this would be a happy day
With no dark dreams remaining from the night,
And no remorse to steal my joy away;

A day in which I feel my spirits soar,
Perceptions heightened, colour bright and clear;
No unknown shadows fall across my floor,
But safety wraps me round and love is near.

*   *   *

I should like to dig a deep dark hole
And lie in it, as if in my bed
And to stretch up high and blot out the sky,
As I pull the grasses over my head.

And to have some peace as my heart-beats cease
With the sound of voices fading away;
And to rest at last with my eyes shut fast,
And wait for my body to turn to clay.

Mary Wilson

SONNET
(Compossed December 1806)

How sweet it is, when mother Fancy rocks
The wayward brain, to saunter through a wood!
An old place, full of many a lovely brood,
Tall trees, green arbours, and ground flowers in flocks;
And wild rose tip-toe upon hawthorn stocks,
Like a bold Girl, who plays her agile pranks
At Wakes and Fairs with wandering Mountebanks,—
When she stands creasting the Clown's head, and mocks
The crowd beneath her. Verily I think,
Such place to me is sometimes a dream
Or map of the whole world: thoughts, link by link,
Enter through ears and eyesight, with such gleam
Of all things, that at last in fear I shrink,
And leap at once from the delicious stream.

William Wordsworth

SONNET
(Compossed 1819)

I Heard (alas! 'twas only in a dream)
Strains—which, as sage Antiquity believed,
By waking ears have sometimes been received
Wafted adown the wind from lake or stream;
A most melodious requiem, a supreme
And perfect harmony of notes, achieved
By a fair Swan on drowsy billows heaved,
O'er which her pinions shed a silver gleam.
For she is not the votary of Apollo?
And knows she not, singing as he inspires,
That bliss awaits her which the ungenial Hallow
Of the dull earth partakes not, nor desires?
Mount, tuneful Bird, and join the immortal quires!
She soared—and I awoke, struggling in vain to follow.

William Wordsworth

*"To make the imperfect perfect
    It is enough to love it"*

>   Kathleen Raine

POETS' BIOGRAPICAL NOTES

BIOGRAPHICAL NOTES

Matthew Arnold (1822-1888), was at Rugby during the headmastership of his father Thomas Arnold and won a schools prize for his poems at the age of 14. He went on to Balliol and won the Newdigate Prize. Needing money, he became an Inspector of Schools while continuing to write.

Richard Bauckham, is Professor of New Testament Studies in the University of St. Andrews, Scotland. He has published twelve books on theological and biblical subjects, and has been writing poetry occasionally for most of his adult life.

William Blake (1757-1827), artist, poet and visionary, was born in London, and married in 1782. He illustrated the works of Thomas Gray and others.

Emily Bronte (1818-1848). Born in Yorkshire the fifth of six children, she lived also in Brussels before returning to Yorkshire to write "Wuthering Heights". Emily's poems were only published under a pseudonym during her life.

Jeremiah Callanan (1795-1846). Born in Cork, he became a pioneer of translating Irish poetry into English, collecting many Irish legends and much folklore. He died in Lisbon.

Margaret Chisman, writes Haiku poetry, which has been published by "The Inquirer" and "Sea of Faith Magazine". As well as being a Director of the Institute of Social Invention, Margaret has written about social development.

Ross Clifford, was born in Hertfordshire and studied painting at the West Sussex Institute before teaching Art, first in Yorkshire and then in Cornwall. Married with two children, Ross is now a free lance writer and artist.

Pamela Constantine founded the Sharkti Laureate imprint, spearhead of the New Renaissance, which promotes a world renaissance of the values that make life meaningful.

George Darling (1795-1846), was educated at Trinty College, Dublin and became a writer for the Theatre in London. His pronouced stammer was considered a reason for the eloquent flow of his poems.

fadma,—mother, gardener, nurse, Sai devotee, Vipassana meditator, Sufi inspired incurable romantic.

Rosemary Goring, was born in Argentina and educated at Roedean and Girton. Rosemary and her husband Jeremy are now in the Christian universalist "Brotherhood of the Cross and Star". Rosemary's poems and songs appear in the last two anthologies of Beyond the Cloister Publications.

John Gurney, read English at Oxford and was a National Poetry Competition prizewinner in 1982, 1991 and 1992. He has been writing poetry and plays full time since 1985 and lives with his wife and family on the South Coast.

Ian Hallett, was a tutor for a correspondence college. A regular walker, swimmer and diarist, Ian drew inspiration from the sea when living on the coast. In recent years he was cared for by his wife Eileen and died in March 1994.

Pamela Harvey, has lived in the Enfield area of Middlesex all her life. After producing several slim volumes of poetry and articals on social history, her continuing hope is of living in a more caring society.

Hugh Hellicar, was a schoolmaster in the 60's before being ordained in the 70's. Most of his poetry has been written while travelling. The care of the elderly is an important part of his ministry and includes Poetry Readings in Nursing Homes.

Robert Herrick (1591-1674) lived in London after graduating at Cambridge. Most of his life was spent as a country parson in Devonshire. His poetry shows the influence of the Latin poets and Ben Jonson..

Philip D. Isaac was born and educated in Yorkshire and worked for ten years in the building trade, but now gives more time to writing poetry and lyrics. His poems appear in " Poems of Faith and Love" (1994).

Eric James, ordained in 1951, was Diocesan Missioner of St. Albans and a Chaplain to Queen Elizabeth 11. He is well known for his leading role in Christian Action and as a broadcaster.

Ben Jonson (1572-1637) was born in London, where he was valued as a playwright and poet. He suffered the separate deaths of a daughter and two sons, and was twice imprisoned. He was buried in Westminster Abbey.

John Keats (1795-1821) born in London, and was 8 when his father died and 14 when his remarried mother died. He became a medical student and qualified, but soon became fully absorbed in writing poetry.

William Kerr(?-?), Little certainly known.

Walter Savage Landor (1775-1864) was born in Warwick and early on became a classicist at Rugby and Oxford.Some of his books were translated from Latin to English. Landor was a friend of Coleridge, Charles Dickens and Robert Browning.

Reg Latham was born and bred in the country, but worked in the City for 25 years. Pacifism and the Society of Friends were strong influences in his life, as well as love of nature. His collection of poems was published after his death in 1988.

James Mangan (1803-1849). Born in Dublin, he became a linguist, but neglected his health and after some years of poverty died of cholera.

Mary Frances Mooney was born in Dublin and moved to London with her family when young. She has written short stories and articles as well as translating the life of Leonie Martin, sister of St. Theresa of Lisieux.

Iris Munns has been writing poetry most of her life, and now lives in Kent, where she has conducted poetry workshops since 1970. She has read poetry on BBC radio.

Arthur O'Shaughnessy (1844-1881) worked in London's Natural History Museum and identified with pre-Raphaelite ideals.

Edgar Allan Poe (1809-1849), born in Boston, Massachusetts and served in the United States army before becoming a journalist and a pioneer of science fiction.

Jack Pollock, Born in Scotland, he lived in South Africa for 10 years where he edited two anthologies. In 1992 he won an award in the McDiarmid Trophy Competition and was given a Diploma of Merit by Ayreshire Poets for his poem "Pablo" in 1995. This poem appears in "Poems of Faith and Love" (1994).

Enoch Powell was Professor of Greek at Sydney University before military service in the last war. An MP for 37 years, Mr. Powell served as a Cabinet Minister and as a Privy Councillor. Four volumes of his poetry have been published.

Maria Rajecka is an artist who experienced a German concentration camp in the last war. Maria is a widow and lives in Brighton. Her poems are written in Polish and English.

Kathleen Raine read Natural Science at Cambridge, won the Harriet Monroe Memorial Prize and was appointed Research Fellow at Girton College. Her books include several on William Blake, some on poetry and twelve volumes of her own poems.

Helen Richards taught English and became headmistress of a school in Oxfordshire. Her love of Oxford and the English language were life long. Miss Richards was a committed Christian and died in 1983.

Christina Rossetti (1830-1894) was a devout Anglican of pre-Rapaelite tendency. She wrote nursery rhymes and poems, some of which became used as hymns.

Frederick Keeling Scott was a country parson in Norfolk before taking a parish in Brighton. He wrote many "place poems", and during retirement encouraged other writers, enabling some to be published.

Percy Shelley (1792-1822). The son of a Sussex baronet, he soon became noted for the ethereal quality of his poetry. He was drowned off Via Reggio at a productive time of writing.

Mary Spain has published four collections of poetry, and won the American 1980 Golden Poets Award. A series of her work has featured on BBC World Service. She shares her London home with Rupert, her boisterous Burmese cat.

Robert Louis Stevenson (1850-1894), born in Edinburgh, was an essayist as well as a writer of fiction and poetry. His work, "A Child's Garden of Verse" was published in 1885.

Alfred, Lord Tennyson (1809-1892). Born in Lincolnshire. In 1850 he married Emily Sellwood and succeeded Wordsworth as Poet Laureate. In 1884 he accepted a peerage.

R.S. Thomas, born in Cardiff, was ordained in 1936 to become a parish priest in rural Wales. His published poems reach over decades and awards include the Queen's Gold Medal for Poetry in 1964. "Neb", his autobiography, was written in Welsh.

Julie Whitby went from Bedales to train for the stage. She appeared in repertory and on TV. Her study of Violette Leduc was published in America, and her own collection of poems "The Violet Room" was published in 1994.

Mary Wilson (nee Baldwin) is the daughter of a clergyman and married Harold, Lord Wilson in 1940. Her several poetry books include experience of State occasions, the Isles of Scilly, love of nature and friendship.

William Wordsworth (1770-1850), born at Cockermouth, he lived for some years in France before returning to England. He became Poet Laureate on his own conditions after the death of his friend Southey.

Late Additions

Thomas Clarkson (1913-1992), spent his early years in Yorkshire before living as a writer and artist in Surrey. A range of published work include novels, short stories and poetry, the most acclaimed novel being "The Pavement and the Sky".

Derek Stanford, was born in rural Middlesex and became a literary journalist. An author and publisher of anthologies, his special interest continues to be poetry of the 1890's.

ACKNOWLEDGEMENTS

Country Life & "Prayer" and "Solo Vision by
Acumen Publications Julie Whitby in "The Violet Room" (1994)

Outposts "Pre-Med" by Iris Munns in Issue 174/5

Golgonooza Press Poems by Kathleen Raine in "Living with Mystery" (1992)

Bellew Publishing Poems in "Collected Poems" Enoch Powell (1990)

Hutchinson and Co. Poems in "New Poems" by Mary Wilson (1979)

Bloodaxe Books &
Macmillian, London Ltd. Poems by R.S. Thomas

Artist

We are most grateful to Roy Clements for his drawing on page 21 which he created specially for this anthology

Notes

"Pit Widow" earned John Gurney a shared First Prize in 1994 City of Cardiff International Poetry Competion.

"Legacy" won Jack Pollock an award in the 1992 MacDiarmid Trophy Competition and appeared in "Poems of Faith and Love" (1994).